DIARY 2009

a wainwright

F
FRANCES LINCOLN LIMITED
PUBLISHERS

Frances Lincoln Limited
4 Torriano Mews
Torriano Avenue
London NW5 2RZ
www.franceslincoln.com

The Wainwright Pocket Diary 2009
Copyright © Frances Lincoln 2008

Illustrations copyright © The Estate of A. Wainwright 1955, 1957, 1960, 1962, 1964, 1974
Astronomical information © Crown Copyright. Reproduced by permission of the Controller
of Her Majesty's Stationery Office and the UK Hydrographic Office (www.ukho.gov.uk)

All rights reserved. No part of this publication may be reproduced, stored in or introduced
into a retrieval system, or transmitted, in any form or by any means (electronic, mechanical,
photocopying, or otherwise), without either prior permission in writing from the publisher or a
licence permitting restricted copying. In the United Kingdom such licences are issued by the
Copyright Licensing Agency, Saffron House, 6–10 Kirby Street, London EC1N 8TS

Printed and bound in China

A CIP catalogue record is available for this book from the British Library.

ISBN: 978-0-7112-2844-3

FRONT COVER:
KNOTT
The Valley of Dale Beck, leading to Roughton Gill
Book 5: The Northern Fells

TITLE PAGE
Drawing taken from Personal Notes
Book 4: The Southern Fells

INTRODUCTION
HARTER FELL
Book 2: The Far Eastern Fells

IMPORTANT NOTE
Pages from A. Wainwright's Pictorial Guides to the Lakeland Fells are used in this diary
for illustration only. Maps and instructions on ascents may therefore not appear here in full.
Walkers who wish to make any of the ascents shown in this diary are strongly advised to
consult the appropriate guide.

GREEN QUARTER FELL The Outlying Fells of Lakeland	NAB SCAR Book 1: The Eastern Fells
DOW CRAG Book 4: The Southern Fells	BINSEY Book 5: The Northern Fells
ARTHUR'S PIKE Book 2: The Far Eastern Fells	WHIN RIGG Book 4: The Southern Fells
CLAIFE HEIGHTS The Outlying Fells of Lakeland	CASTLE CRAG Book 6: The North Western Fells
GREAT COCKUP Book 5: The Northern Fells	BAKESTALL Book 5: The Northern Fells
HARTSOP DODD Book 2: The Far Eastern Fells	OUTERSIDE Book 6: The North Western Fells

2009

January
M	T	W	T	F	S	S
			1	2	3	4
5	6	7	8	9	10	11
12	13	14	15	16	17	18
19	20	21	22	23	24	25
26	27	28	29	30	31	

February
M	T	W	T	F	S	S
						1
2	3	4	5	6	7	8
9	10	11	12	13	14	15
16	17	18	19	20	21	22
23	24	25	26	27	28	

March
M	T	W	T	F	S	S
						1
2	3	4	5	6	7	8
9	10	11	12	13	14	15
16	17	18	19	20	21	22
23	24	25	26	27	28	29
30	31					

April
M	T	W	T	F	S	S
		1	2	3	4	5
6	7	8	9	10	11	12
13	14	15	16	17	18	19
20	21	22	23	24	25	26
27	28	29	30			

May
M	T	W	T	F	S	S
				1	2	3
4	5	6	7	8	9	10
11	12	13	14	15	16	17
18	19	20	21	22	23	24
25	26	27	28	29	30	31

June
M	T	W	T	F	S	S
1	2	3	4	5	6	7
8	9	10	11	12	13	14
15	16	17	18	19	20	21
22	23	24	25	26	27	28
29	30					

July
M	T	W	T	F	S	S
		1	2	3	4	5
6	7	8	9	10	11	12
13	14	15	16	17	18	19
20	21	22	23	24	25	26
27	28	29	30	31		

August
M	T	W	T	F	S	S
					1	2
3	4	5	6	7	8	9
10	11	12	13	14	15	16
17	18	19	20	21	22	23
24	25	26	27	28	29	30
31						

September
M	T	W	T	F	S	S
	1	2	3	4	5	6
7	8	9	10	11	12	13
14	15	16	17	18	19	20
21	22	23	24	25	26	27
28	29	30				

October
M	T	W	T	F	S	S
			1	2	3	4
5	6	7	8	9	10	11
12	13	14	15	16	17	18
19	20	21	22	23	24	25
26	27	28	29	30	31	

November
M	T	W	T	F	S	S
						1
2	3	4	5	6	7	8
9	10	11	12	13	14	15
16	17	18	19	20	21	22
23	24	25	26	27	28	29
30						

December
M	T	W	T	F	S	S
	1	2	3	4	5	6
7	8	9	10	11	12	13
14	15	16	17	18	19	20
21	22	23	24	25	26	27
28	29	30	31			

2010

January
M	T	W	T	F	S	S
				1	2	3
4	5	6	7	8	9	10
11	12	13	14	15	16	17
18	19	20	21	22	23	24
25	26	27	28	29	30	31

February
M	T	W	T	F	S	S
1	2	3	4	5	6	7
8	9	10	11	12	13	14
15	16	17	18	19	20	21
22	23	24	25	26	27	28

March
M	T	W	T	F	S	S
1	2	3	4	5	6	7
8	9	10	11	12	13	14
15	16	17	18	19	20	21
22	23	24	25	26	27	28
29	30	31				

April
M	T	W	T	F	S	S
			1	2	3	4
5	6	7	8	9	10	11
12	13	14	15	16	17	18
19	20	21	22	23	24	25
26	27	28	29	30		

May
M	T	W	T	F	S	S
					1	2
3	4	5	6	7	8	9
10	11	12	13	14	15	16
17	18	19	20	21	22	23
24	25	26	27	28	29	30
31						

June
M	T	W	T	F	S	S
	1	2	3	4	5	6
7	8	9	10	11	12	13
14	15	16	17	18	19	20
21	22	23	24	25	26	27
28	29	30				

July
M	T	W	T	F	S	S
			1	2	3	4
5	6	7	8	9	10	11
12	13	14	15	16	17	18
19	20	21	22	23	24	25
26	27	28	29	30	31	

August
M	T	W	T	F	S	S
						1
2	3	4	5	6	7	8
9	10	11	12	13	14	15
16	17	18	19	20	21	22
23	24	25	26	27	28	29
30	31					

September
M	T	W	T	F	S	S
		1	2	3	4	5
6	7	8	9	10	11	12
13	14	15	16	17	18	19
20	21	22	23	24	25	26
27	28	29	30			

October
M	T	W	T	F	S	S
				1	2	3
4	5	6	7	8	9	10
11	12	13	14	15	16	17
18	19	20	21	22	23	24
25	26	27	28	29	30	31

November
M	T	W	T	F	S	S
1	2	3	4	5	6	7
8	9	10	11	12	13	14
15	16	17	18	19	20	21
22	23	24	25	26	27	28
29	30					

December
M	T	W	T	F	S	S
		1	2	3	4	5
6	7	8	9	10	11	12
13	14	15	16	17	18	19
20	21	22	23	24	25	26
27	28	29	30	31		

ALFRED WAINWRIGHT AND THE PICTORIAL GUIDES TO THE LAKELAND FELLS

The pages used to illustrate this pocket diary come from the Pictorial Guides to the Lakeland Fells and *The Outlying Fells of Lakeland* created by A. Wainwright, the legendary author, artist and fellwalker. Originally compiled in the 1950s and early 1960s, Wainwright's Pictorial Guides are surely the most distinctive and unusual walking guides ever. They contain vivid descriptions of the fells he loved, intricate pen-and-ink sketches, detailed maps of ascents and ridge walks and, of course, pithy words of advice for walkers who follow in his footsteps. *The Outlying Fells of Lakeland* was published later in 1974 and follows the same style.

Born in Blackburn in 1907, Wainwright left school at the age of thirteen to work as an office boy in the Borough Engineer's office. Years of evening classes followed while he studied for his professional qualifications as an accountant. A holiday to the Lake District at the age of twenty-three changed his life by kindling a lifelong passion for the fells. In 1941 he was offered a post in Kendal, where he subsequently rose to become a popular Borough Treasurer. From then on he devoted every spare minute of his days to researching and compiling the original seven Pictorial Guides. After the last of these appeared in 1966, further Pictorial Guides followed, along with twenty-nine books of sketches of different regions of England, Scotland and Wales. In 1974 he became Chairman of Animal Rescue, Cumbria, and thanks to the book royalties he contributed to the charity, a permanent animal shelter was established near Kendal.

A. Wainwright died in 1991 at the age of eighty-four.

Haweswater
from the third cairn

Green Quarter Fell

visiting
 Hollow Moor, 1394'
 a nameless summit, 1370'
with a detour to
 Skeggles Water
1000 feet of ascent

from KENTMERE CHURCH

4¾ miles

3 hours

(4 miles,
 2½ hours,
 omitting
 the detour)

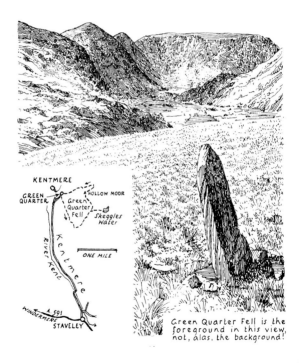

Green Quarter Fell is the foreground in this view, not, alas, the background!

WEEK 1

DECEMBER/JANUARY

29 MONDAY

30 TUESDAY

31 WEDNESDAY   New Year's Eve

1 THURSDAY   New Year's Day
                              Holiday, UK, Republic of Ireland, Canada,
                                    USA, Australia and New Zealand

2 FRIDAY   Holiday, Scotland and New Zealand

3 SATURDAY

4 SUNDAY   *First Quarter*

WEEK 2

JANUARY

5 MONDAY

6 TUESDAY   Epiphany

7 WEDNESDAY

8 THURSDAY

9 FRIDAY

10 SATURDAY

11 SUNDAY   *Full Moon*

Green Quarter Fell is the featureless grassy height overlooking the hamlet of Kentmere to the east, and walkers in the valley invariably turn their backs on it and proceed to the fine surround of hills ahead, as indeed they should if they have youth on their side — for Green Quarter Fell has nothing to compare with the broad acres of High Street or the rough ridges leading thereto. Yet this modest fell, though rarely visited, has one thing the others lack — a perfectly-balanced and lovely view of upper Kentmere, best seen from the path used in descent, that cries aloud for a camera.
This apart, the long easy climb is without excitement and its accomplishment is gratifying only as evidence that there is life in the old dog yet.

The start of the bridleway

Skeggles Water from the bridleway

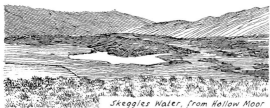

Skeggles Water, from Hollow Moor

Skeggles Water, lying in a vast bowl of heather, is conveniently visited on this walk but is an uninviting place with attractions mainly for bird-watchers and anglers. A few years ago a proposal to exploit the tarn for diatomite was defeated by concerted objections from local people and amenity societies.

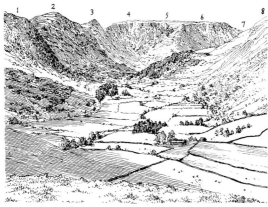

Upper Kentmere, as seen on the descent

1 : Rainsborrow Crag
2 : Ill Bell
3 : Froswick
4 : Thornthwaite Crag
5 : High Street
6 : Mardale Ill Bell
7 : Nan Bield Pass
8 : slopes of Harter Fell

WEEK 3

JANUARY

12 MONDAY

13 TUESDAY

14 WEDNESDAY

15 THURSDAY

16 FRIDAY

17 SATURDAY

18 SUNDAY *Last Quarter*

WEEK 4

JANUARY

19 MONDAY Holiday, USA (Martin Luther King's Birthday)

20 TUESDAY

21 WEDNESDAY

22 THURSDAY

23 FRIDAY

24 SATURDAY

25 SUNDAY

MAP

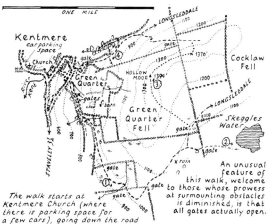

The walk starts at Kentmere Church (where there is parking space for a few cars), going down the road to Low Bridge and there turning up a side road to the hamlet of Green Quarter, cutting off a loop by a signposted footpath. Or, to avoid the steep pull up to Green Quarter, a car may be parked among the buildings there, with permission, or a walker may be dropped at this point for collection later.

Two signposts are prominent on the roadside here — one says 'Footpath to Longsleddale (Sadgill)' and is our route of return; the other, 100 yards south, says 'Bridleway to Longsleddale via Cocklaw Fell' and the outward route goes through a gate here (the first of many). The bridleway is initially unenclosed but soon runs between walls. When the wall on the left turns uphill take the branch path following it and cross a stream. Now the route is clearly defined for the next mile, the path climbing gradually and curving round the fellside in a wide loop to bring Skeggles Water into sight. Beyond a ruin the path bifurcates, the more obvious branch heading directly for a gate in a wall admitting to Skeggles Water, which may now be visited. Then resume the bridleway, leaving it after the next gate to ascend the easy grass slope half-left and so reach the top of the fell, which is adorned with a stone gatepost and has a superb view of the head of Kentmere. Continue by curving east along the ridge to a cross-fence, simply negotiated by cocking one leg over and then the other. Just beyond, in tussocky grass, is a secondary summit (no cairn), from which descend the north slope to join an old cart-track that goes down gently to Green Quarter. Take your time along this easy terrace and enjoy one of the most beautiful views in Lakeland.

Dow Crag 2555'

from the Cove

GREY FRIAR SWIRL HOW
Troutal CONISTON OLD MAN
DOW CRAG Coniston
Seathwaite
MILES
0 1 2 3

WEEK 5

JANUARY/FEBRUARY

26 MONDAY *New Moon*
Chinese New Year
Holiday, Australia (Australia Day)

27 TUESDAY

28 WEDNESDAY

29 THURSDAY

30 FRIDAY

31 SATURDAY

1 SUNDAY

WEEK 6

FEBRUARY

2 MONDAY *First Quarter*

3 TUESDAY

4 WEDNESDAY

5 THURSDAY

6 FRIDAY Holiday, New Zealand (Waitangi Day)
Accession of Queen Elizabeth II

7 SATURDAY

8 SUNDAY

Dow Crag 4

Cove Bridge carries the Walna Scar 'road' (a green path) across Torver Beck

The big cave, Blind Tarn Quarry

A shelter alongside the Walna Scar road, east of the pass, just big enough for one person or a honeymoon couple

Brown Pike and Blind Tarn from Buck Pike

Brown Pike has a fine cairn. Blind Tarn is one of the few tarns without an outlet — hence its name.

Dow Crag 7

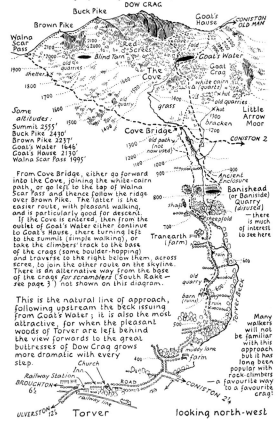

ASCENT FROM TORVER
2250 feet of ascent: 3¾ miles

Some altitudes:
Summit 2555'
Buck Pike 2430'
Brown Pike 2237'
Goat's Water 1646'
Goat's Hause 2130'
Walna Scar Pass 1995'

From Cove Bridge, either go forward into the Cove, joining the white-cairn path, or go left to the top of Walna Scar Pass and thence follow the ridge over Brown Pike. The latter is the easier route, with pleasant walking, and is particularly good for descent.
If the Cove is entered, then from the outlet of Goat's Water either continue to Goat's Hause, there turning left to the summit (simple walking), or take the climbers' track to the base of the crags (some boulder-hopping) and traverse to the right below them, across scree, to join the other route on the skyline. There is an alternative way from the base of the crags for scramblers (South Rake — see page 3) not shown on this diagram.

This is the natural line of approach, following upstream the beck issuing from Goat's Water; it is also the most attractive, for when the pleasant woods of Torver are left behind the view forwards to the great buttresses of Dow Crag grows more dramatic with every step.

Many walkers will not be familiar with this approach but it has long been popular with rock-climbers — a favourite way to a favourite crag!

Torver

looking north-west

WEEK 7

FEBRUARY

9 MONDAY	*Full Moon*

10 TUESDAY

11 WEDNESDAY

12 THURSDAY	Holiday, USA (Lincoln's Birthday)

13 FRIDAY

14 SATURDAY	St. Valentine's Day

15 SUNDAY

WEEK 8

FEBRUARY

---

16 MONDAY *Last Quarter*
Holiday, USA (Washington's Birthday)

---

17 TUESDAY

---

18 WEDNESDAY

---

19 THURSDAY

---

20 FRIDAY

---

21 SATURDAY

---

22 SUNDAY

Dow Crag 12

Dow Crag from Goat's Water

Arthur's Pike 1747'

from the Howtown road

- Pooley Bridge
- Askham
- ▲ ARTHUR'S PIKE
- Howtown
- ▲ LOADPOT HILL

WEEK 9

FEBRUARY/MARCH

23 MONDAY

24 TUESDAY   Shrove Tuesday

25 WEDNESDAY   *New Moon*
                                                     Ash Wednesday

26 THURSDAY

27 FRIDAY

28 SATURDAY

1 SUNDAY   St. David's Day

WEEK 10

MARCH

2 MONDAY

3 TUESDAY

4 WEDNESDAY   *First Quarter*

5 THURSDAY

6 FRIDAY

7 SATURDAY

8 SUNDAY

Arthur's Pike 2

NATURAL FEATURES

Arthur's Pike is the northerly termination of the long High Street range, and, like the northerly termination of the parallel Helvellyn range, it contrasts with the usual Lakeland fell-structure by exhibiting its crags to the afternoon sun; the northern and eastern slopes, which are commonly roughest, are without rock. The steep flank falling to Ullswater has several faces of crag below the summit-rim, and, especially around the vicinity of Swarthbeck Gill, which forms the southern boundary of the fell, acres of tumbled boulders testify to the roughness of the impending cliffs and the power of the beck in flood. Above the crags, there is little to excite, and the summit merges without much change in elevation into the broad expanses of Loadpot Hill. The gradual northern slope is clothed with heather.

MAP

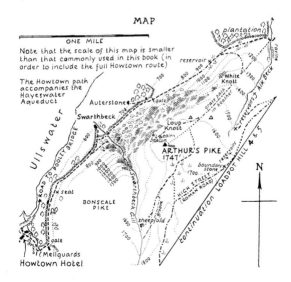

Arthur's Pike 3

Ullswater, from the Howtown path

ASCENTS

Arthur's Pike looks particularly forbidding from the Howtown path, by which it is usually climbed, and the timid walker who doubts the wisdom of proceeding will be reassured to discover that the ascent is not only not intimidating but surprisingly easy and everywhere pleasant, *if the route shown on the map is followed*. The obvious and direct alternative by the Swarthbeck ravine is anything but obvious and direct when attempted, and nervous pedestrians should keep away from it.

For the approaches from Askham, Helton and Pooley Bridge, the chapter on Loadpot Hill should be consulted.

THE SUMMIT

Above the edge of the steep Ullswater flank, grassy undulations culminate in a conical knoll crowned by a large cairn; nearby is a shelter (from wind) in a short wall. There are no paths on the top, but an indefinite cairned track skirts the precipice, on the brink of which is a collapsed beacon; and on the eastern side is a fairly good path that goes nowhere in particular in either direction and is of little use to the walker. The beacon cannot be seen from the summit-cairn; it stands 250 yards distant in the direction of Blencathra.

WEEK 11

MARCH

9 MONDAY   Commonwealth Day

10 TUESDAY

11 WEDNESDAY   *Full Moon*

12 THURSDAY

13 FRIDAY

14 SATURDAY

15 SUNDAY

Arthur's Pike 5

RIDGE ROUTES

To LOADPOT HILL, 2201': 2¼ miles
S, then SSW, SSE and finally N
Minor depressions : 500 feet of ascent
A dull, easy walk, not recommended in mist

Aim for the low hill due south, crossing a good path on the way, and join there the old High Street, which is now indistinct in places and at its best only a series of ruts in the grass, often marshy. When the dome of Loadpot Hill is reached, the path becomes an ascending groove, easy to follow; it turns away downhill just short of the ruins of Lowther House, where turn north to the summit cairn, which encloses a boundary stone. *This is not a walk for a wet day, and the whole of this moorland is a nightmare in mist.*

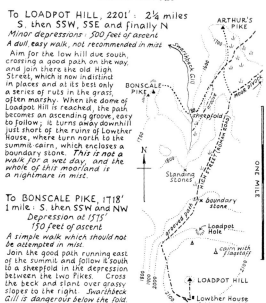

To BONSCALE PIKE, 1718'
1 mile: S. then SSW and NW
Depression at 1575'
150 feet of ascent

A simple walk which should not be attempted in mist.

Join the good path running east of the summit and follow it south to a sheepfold in the depression between the two Pikes. Cross the beck and slant over grassy slopes to the right. *Swarthbeck Gill is dangerous below the fold.*

Ullswater, from the beacon

WEEK 12

MARCH

16 MONDAY

17 TUESDAY — St. Patrick's Day
Holiday, Northern Ireland and Republic of Ireland

18 WEDNESDAY — *Last Quarter*

19 THURSDAY

20 FRIDAY — Vernal Equinox

21 SATURDAY

22 SUNDAY — Mothering Sunday, UK

WEEK 13

MARCH

23 MONDAY

24 TUESDAY

25 WEDNESDAY

26 THURSDAY *New Moon*

27 FRIDAY

28 SATURDAY

29 SUNDAY British Summer Time begins

Arthur's Pike 6

Swarthbeck Gill

Swarthbeck Gill, if it were but more accessible, would be one of the showplaces of the district. Here, between towering rockwalls, are beautiful cataracts, but, alas, they are out of the reach of the average explorer. The fern, tree-clad lower gorge, however, may (and should) be visited. The prudent venture no further!

Claife Heights

No definite summit.
Highest parts
about 900'.

500 feet of ascent

from FAR SAWREY
5 miles
3 hours

from Esthwaite Water

WEEK 14

MARCH/APRIL

30 MONDAY

31 TUESDAY

1 WEDNESDAY

2 THURSDAY *First Quarter*

3 FRIDAY

4 SATURDAY

5 SUNDAY Palm Sunday

WEEK 15

APRIL

6 MONDAY

7 TUESDAY

8 WEDNESDAY

9 THURSDAY
Full Moon
Maundy Thursday
Passover (Pesach), First Day

10 FRIDAY
Good Friday
Holiday, UK, Canada, USA, Australia and New Zealand

11 SATURDAY

12 SUNDAY
Easter Day

Claife Heights is the naturally-wooded and man-afforested upland rising between Esthwaite Water and Windermere. It has not a well-defined summit, the highest point (about 900 feet, north of Pale Crags) having an Ordnance column now lost in conifers and inaccessible, as indeed is most of this upland where Beatrix Potter loved to wander. Its best feature is a series of tarns in lovely settings: reservoirs actually but not obtrusively artificial; none of them appears on 19th century maps. The most attractive of these is Moss Eccles Tarn, which has a glimpse of Windermere and is a charming spot for a siesta. Wise Een Tarn is more open and has a view to the Langdales. Three Dubs Tarn is deeply inurned in a surround of tall trees, and shy: it has a boat-house, better built than most.

Claife Heights is delightful. It was more so before forestry curtailed walking and restricted the views.

Moss Eccles Tarn

Wise Een Tarn

It matters little whether the walk is commenced at Near or Far Sawrey but as the finish is at the latter village it is more convenient to make it the starting point. There is limited roadside parking near the telephone kiosk.

Take the tarmac lane rising on the west side of the Sawrey Hotel, leaving it by a path forking left beyond a cattle grid. Cross a stream (watercress here) and enter a gated lane to join a rough road coming up from Near Sawrey. Follow this to a gate below Moss Eccles Tarn, whence it continues over open ground as a cart-track and, skirting Wise Een Tarn, becomes a less distinct footpath rising into the forest ahead, where it assumes the dimensions of a forest road. At a hairpin bend, a small sign, not very conspicuous, and arrowed H and W (which presumably stand for Hawkshead and Wray) indicates a path going off to the right between the trees (Grass of Parnassus grows alongside it). This is where the fun starts. The way soon becomes distinct underfoot and, in an amazing journey, which in its course zigzags to all points of the compass, enters dense forest. White splashes of paint waymark the path, which is a desperate passage through encroaching and overhanging spruce in many places. At two rocky outcrops, unplanted, there are merciful respites and open views: the first of the Ambleside district and the second, on Pate Crags, of Moss Eccles Tarn and Wise Een Tarn, with Three Dubs Tarn directly below and almost hidden by conifers. Ultimately, just as hope is fading, the old path to Belle Grange from Sawrey is joined at a small signpost and troubles are over. Turn right. The path enters a cart-track and leads back into Far Sawrey (a branch going off to the Windermere Ferry) by the lane coming down on the east side of the hotel.

In 1972 the trees fringing the forest path referred to above were in sad need of pruning. By 1974, failing this attention the path will be impassable. If difficulty and discomfort is experienced, complain to the Forestry Office at Grizedale.

Three Dubs Tarn

(on private ground)

WEEK 16

APRIL

13 MONDAY
Easter Monday
Holiday, UK (exc. Scotland), Republic of Ireland,
Canada, Australia and New Zealand

14 TUESDAY

15 WEDNESDAY
Passover (Pesach), Seventh Day

16 THURSDAY
Passover (Pesach), Eighth Day

17 FRIDAY
Last Quarter

18 SATURDAY

19 SUNDAY

WEEK 17

APRIL

20 MONDAY

21 TUESDAY Birthday of Queen Elizabeth II

22 WEDNESDAY

23 THURSDAY St. George's Day

24 FRIDAY *New Moon*
Holiday, Australia and New Zealand (Anzac Day)

25 SATURDAY

26 SUNDAY

MAP

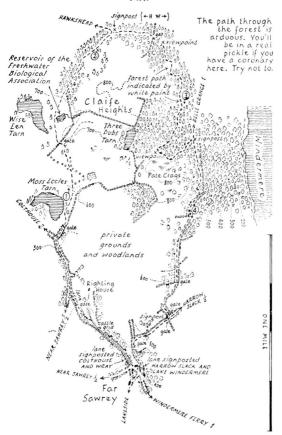

Great Cockup

1720' approx

from Longlands

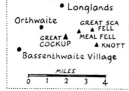

Orthwaite Hall

WEEK 18

APRIL/MAY

27 MONDAY

28 TUESDAY

29 WEDNESDAY

30 THURSDAY

1 FRIDAY   *First Quarter*

2 SATURDAY

3 SUNDAY

WEEK 19

MAY

4 MONDAY Early Spring Bank Holiday, UK and Republic of Ireland

5 TUESDAY

6 WEDNESDAY

7 THURSDAY

8 FRIDAY

9 SATURDAY *Full Moon*

10 SUNDAY Mother's Day, USA, Canada, Australia and New Zealand

Great Cockup 2

NATURAL FEATURES

Viewed from a distance, Great Cockup appears as a modest but extensive eminence with no obvious summit and nothing calling for closer inspection. First impressions are confirmed by a tour of exploration, the fell underfoot proving no more attractive than the fell at a distance. Bracken is rampant on the lower slopes, much burning of heather has resulted in a dark and patchy appearance higher up, and the skyline never bestirs itself from placid curves to produce even the slightest excitement. Although not ornamental, however, Great Cockup is strongly functional, which perhaps matters more: its long spine, rising steeply from Orthwaite, divides the waters of the River Ellen from those of tributaries of the Derwent. The fell terminates abruptly in the deep cut of Trusmadoor; beyond, a ridge continues the height of land over Meal Fell to the major summit of the Uldale group, Great Sca Fell.

A feature of the south flank of Great Cockup and always conspicuous on a bright day is the white-streaked *Brockle Crag*. This is disappointing on close inspection, being no more than an untidy fall of quartzite rocks.

Brockle Crag

The Boulder
(Burn Tod behind)

The Boulder. On the Ordnance map of scale 6" = 1 mile there is inscribed the word 'Boulder' at a point alongside the old bridleway crossing the south flank of Great Cockup — a distinction so rare that a walker of an enquiring turn of mind must needs go in search of this natural wonder. Finding it is easy — it stands in isolation — but its dimensions are rather a disappointment, none exceeding a few feet. There are thousands of bigger specimens within a mile of Sty Head. This recording of an ordinary stone illustrates the dearth of features on the fell.

The boulder may be the debris of a now-vanished crag but its situation suggests that it is more probably an erratic left by a retreating glacier.

WEEK 20

MAY

---

11 MONDAY

---

12 TUESDAY

---

13 WEDNESDAY

---

14 THURSDAY

---

15 FRIDAY

---

16 SATURDAY

---

17 SUNDAY *Last Quarter*

Great Cockup 4

ASCENT FROM ORTHWAITE
950 feet of ascent : 2 miles

The summit is easily reached from the highest part of the old bridle-way, up a simple slope of grass and heather, the true summit being 300 yards beyond the cairned top first gained, just above the shooting butts. This route is better than a direct climb up Orthwaite Bank, where the bracken is dense and extensive. For a different route of return, go down the far slope to Trusmadoor and then use sheep-tracks alongside Burntod Gill; a further variation, crossing marshy ground, passes below Brockle Crag and joins the farm-road.

The Dash Valley

Great Cockup 5

THE SUMMIT

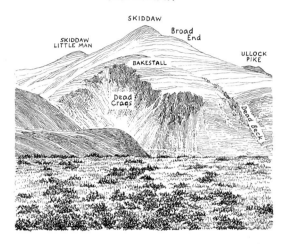

A visitor here must do his own surveying to determine the highest point, there being no cairn on it, but, subject to a difference of opinion of a few yards, all will agree it is in the midst of an expanse of scanty, anaemic-looking heather on the crest of a gentle dome. 300 yards west is a more definite top with a few stones, but this is quite obviously lower. Nearer, north-east, there is also a cairn on a rise: this, too, is lower.

On the 6" Ordnance map three surface-levels are given —1690, 1673 and 1701. The heights of 1690 and 1701 would seem to apply to the two tops with cairns. The highest point must be in the middle of the wide 1700' contour on the 2½" map; there is no 1725 contour and the true altitude of the fell may reasonably be taken to be around 1720'.

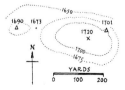

DESCENTS may safely be made in any direction, a little care being necessary in bad weather in the neighbourhood of Trusmadoor, where there are small cliffs.

WEEK 21

MAY

18 MONDAY   Holiday, Canada (Victoria Day)

19 TUESDAY

20 WEDNESDAY

21 THURSDAY   Ascension Day

22 FRIDAY

23 SATURDAY

24 SUNDAY   *New Moon*

WEEK 22

MAY

25 MONDAY Spring Bank Holiday, UK
Holiday, USA (Memorial Day)

26 TUESDAY

27 WEDNESDAY

28 THURSDAY

29 FRIDAY Feast of Weeks (Shavuot)

30 SATURDAY

31 SUNDAY *First Quarter*
Whit Sunday (Pentecost)

Great Cockup 6

THE VIEW

Great Cockup is the most westerly of the Uldale Fells and thus has an unrestricted view across to the Solway Firth and Scotland, which deserves more attention than the rather unattractive mountain scene. Nevertheless the undisputed monarch in this picture is Skiddaw, rising magnificently nearby in the south.

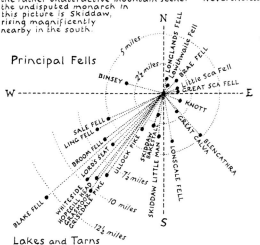

Principal Fells

Lakes and Tarns

WSW: Bassenthwaite Lake
Over Water (NW) cannot be seen from the highest point, but is in view from the two cairned tops.

RIDGE ROUTE

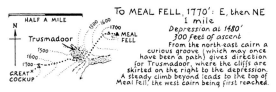

To MEAL FELL, 1770': E, then NE
1 mile
Depression at 1480'
300 feet of ascent

From the north-east cairn a curious groove (which may once have been a path) gives direction for Trusmadoor, where the cliffs are skirted on the right to the depression. A steady climb beyond leads to the top of Meal Fell, the west cairn being first reached.

Hartsop Dodd 2018'

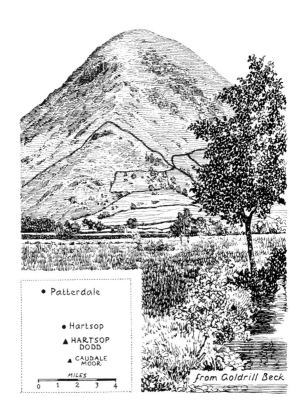

WEEK 23

JUNE

1 MONDAY   Holiday, Republic of Ireland
                  Holiday, New Zealand (Queen's Birthday)

2 TUESDAY   Coronation Day

3 WEDNESDAY

4 THURSDAY

5 FRIDAY

6 SATURDAY

7 SUNDAY   *Full Moon*
                                              Trinity Sunday

WEEK 24

JUNE

8 MONDAY

9 TUESDAY

10 WEDNESDAY

11 THURSDAY   Corpus Christi

12 FRIDAY

13 SATURDAY   The Queen's Official Birthday

14 SUNDAY

Hartsop Dodd 2

NATURAL FEATURES

For a few miles along the road from Patterdale to Kirkstone, Hartsop Dodd has the form of a steepsided conical hill, rising like a giant tumulus from the flat floor of the valley; a high ridge connecting with the loftier Caudale Moor behind is unseen and unsuspected. After the fashion of many subsidiary fells in this area, the imposing front is a sham, for the Dodd is no more than the knuckled fist at the end of one of the several arms of Caudale Moor. It rises from pleasant places, pastures and woods and water, and quite rightly has been named from the delightful hamlet nestling unspoilt among trees at its foot.

It is interesting to note that Hartsop Dodd (*Low* Hartsop Dodd) has a greater elevation than its counterpart *High* Hartsop Dodd nearby, the prefixes relating to their geographical positions in the valley, not to their altitudes

The word 'Low' is usually omitted in references to Hartsop village

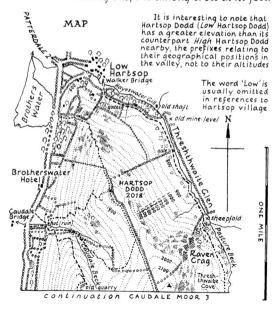

Hartsop Dodd 3

ASCENTS

A feature of the paths leading up Hartsop Dodd is that, for much of their length, they run in well-engineered grooves that help considerably in defining the routes. The best way up is by the steep north ridge, a beautiful climb. The path zigzagging up the west flank is also steep, and rather dreary. The only easy route follows Caudale Beck at first and ultimately gains the ridge between the Dodd and Caudale Moor; this way is dull.

THE SUMMIT

A wall crosses the grassy top, the highest point being indicated by a wooden fence-post against the wall from which a fence formerly went down the fellside. A few stones fallen from the wall at its first bend southwards have been piled together to form a cairn of no significance.

DESCENTS: The grooves do not continue onto the summit. To find the path going down to the west, walk in the direction of Dove Crag, passing by two more fence-posts minus fence — the top of the groove is just beyond the second. To find the path down the north ridge towards Ullswater — the groove starts soon after the ground steepens; keep to the ridge and avoid the parallel gully on the right. The longer easy route is scarcely worth consideration.

In mist, the path on the west will be easiest to find — leave the top fence-post at right angles to the wall and look for the other two which give the key to the descent.

To CAUDALE MOOR, 2502'
1½ miles : SSE, then S
Depression at 1900' : 620 feet of ascent

An easy climb on grass, safe in mist. The wall drearily links the two summits. In fine weather, interest may be introduced into the walk by following the edge of the escarpment on the left, the views therefrom down into Threshthwaite being very striking.

WEEK 25

JUNE

15 MONDAY
Last Quarter
St. Swithin's Day

16 TUESDAY

17 WEDNESDAY

18 THURSDAY

19 FRIDAY

20 SATURDAY

21 SUNDAY
Summer Solstice
Father's Day, UK, Canada and USA

WEEK 26

JUNE

22 MONDAY   New Moon

23 TUESDAY

24 WEDNESDAY

25 THURSDAY

26 FRIDAY

27 SATURDAY

28 SUNDAY

Hartsop Dodd 6

Nab Scar　　　　　　　　　　1450'

▲ FAIRFIELD

▲ GREAT RIGG

▲ STONE ARTHUR

▲ HERON PIKE

● Grasmere ▲ NAB SCAR
　　　　　● Rydal

Ambleside ●

MILES
0　1　2　3　4

from Rydal Water

WEEK 27

JUNE/JULY

29 MONDAY *First Quarter*

30 TUESDAY

1 WEDNESDAY Holiday, Canada (Canada Day)

2 THURSDAY

3 FRIDAY Holiday, USA (Independence Day)

4 SATURDAY Independence Day, USA

5 SUNDAY

WEEK 28

JULY

6 MONDAY

7 TUESDAY   *Full Moon*

8 WEDNESDAY

9 THURSDAY

10 FRIDAY

11 SATURDAY

12 SUNDAY

Nab Scar 2

NATURAL FEATURES

Nab Scar is well known. Its associations with the Lake Poets who came to dwell at the foot of its steep wooded slopes have invested it with romance, and its commanding position overlooking Rydal Water brings it to the notice of the many visitors to that charming lake. It is a fine abrupt height, with a rough, craggy south face; on the flanks are easier slopes. Elevated ground continues beyond the summit and rises gently to Heron Pike. Nab Scar is not a separate fell, but is merely the butt of the long southern ridge of Fairfield.

MAP

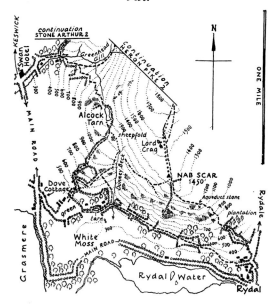

Nab Scar 3

ASCENTS

The popular ascent is from Rydal, a charming climb along a good path, steep in its middle reaches; this is the beginning of the 'Fairfield Horseshoe' when it is walked clockwise. The path from Grasmere is much less used and is not easy to trace in its later stages but this is of no consequence in clear weather.

THE SUMMIT

Strictly, Nab Scar is the name of the craggy south face, not of the fell rising above it, but its recognised summit is a tall edifice of stones built well back from the edge of the cliffs, near a crumbled wall that runs north towards Heron Pike. Hereabouts the immediate surroundings are uninteresting, the redeeming feature being the fine view.

Nab Scar has a subterranean watercourse: below its surface the Thirlmere aqueduct runs through a tunnel. The scars of this operation are nearly gone, but evidence of the existence of the tunnel remains alongside the Rydal path, above the steepest part: here may be found a block of stone a yard square set in the ground; it bears no inscription but marks the position of the tunnel directly beneath.

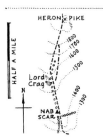

RIDGE ROUTE

To HERON PIKE, 2003': ⅔ mile : N
570 feet of ascent
An easy climb on grass
A plain path accompanies the old wall.
When it forks, either track may be taken

WEEK 29

JULY

13 MONDAY   Battle of the Boyne
                                                  Holiday, Northern Ireland

14 TUESDAY

15 WEDNESDAY   *Last Quarter*

16 THURSDAY

17 FRIDAY

18 SATURDAY

19 SUNDAY

WEEK 30

JULY

20 MONDAY

21 TUESDAY

22 WEDNESDAY *New Moon*

23 THURSDAY

24 FRIDAY

25 SATURDAY

26 SUNDAY

Nab Scar 4

THE VIEW

Principal Fells

This is an 'unbalanced' view, most of it being exceptionally dull, the rest exceptionally charming. Lakes and tarns are a very special feature of the delightful prospect to south and west and the grouping of the Coniston and Langdale fells is quite attractive.

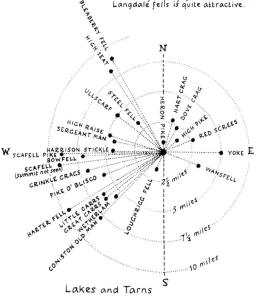

Lakes and Tarns

SSE :	Windermere
S :	Blelham Tarn
S :	Esthwaite Water
SSW :	Coniston Water
SW :	Elterwater
WSW :	Grasmere
WNW :	Easedale Tarn
NW :	Alcock Tarn

Binsey 1466'

from Robin Hood, near Bassenthwaite

Private path in Binsey Plantation

WEEK 31

JULY/AUGUST

27 MONDAY

28 TUESDAY							*First Quarter*

29 WEDNESDAY

30 THURSDAY

31 FRIDAY

1 SATURDAY

2 SUNDAY

WEEK 32

AUGUST

3 MONDAY Summer Bank Holiday, Scotland
Holiday, Republic of Ireland

4 TUESDAY

5 WEDNESDAY

6 THURSDAY *Full Moon*

7 FRIDAY

8 SATURDAY

9 SUNDAY

Binsey 2

NATURAL FEATURES

Binsey is the odd man out. This gentle hill rises beyond the circular perimeter of the Northern Fells, detached and solitary, like a dunce set apart from the class. It is of no great height, is well within the category of Sunday afternoon strolls, has an easy slope just right for exercising the dog or the children, is without precipices and pitfalls, never killed or injured anybody, breeds hares instead of foxes, and is generally of benign appearance. Yet it is much too good to be omitted from these pages.

For one thing it is a most excellent station for appraising the Northern Fells as a preliminary to their exploration. For another, it is a viewpoint of outstanding merit. For another, it possesses a grand little summit with a once-important but now-forgotten history. For another, its rocks are volcanic, not slate as are those of all neighbour fells.

Binsey occupies the extreme north-west corner of the Lake District. Beyond is the coastal plain, then the sea, then Scotland; nothing intervenes to interrupt this sweeping panorama. What a domain, and what a throne to view it from!

the summit ridge, looking east

West Crag

Binsey 5

ASCENT FROM BINSEY LODGE
620 feet of ascent : 1 mile

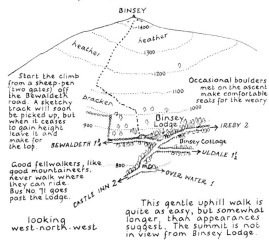

Start the climb from a sheep-pen (two gates) off the Bewaldeth road. A sketchy track will soon be picked up, but when it ceases to gain height leave it and make for the top.

Occasional boulders met on the ascent make comfortable seats for the weary

Good fellwalkers, like good mountaineers, never walk where they can ride. Bus No. 71 goes past the Lodge.

looking west-north-west

This gentle uphill walk is quite as easy, but somewhat longer, than appearances suggest. The summit is not in view from Binsey Lodge.

Binsey Lodge

WEEK 33

AUGUST

10 MONDAY

11 TUESDAY

12 WEDNESDAY

13 THURSDAY *Last Quarter*

14 FRIDAY

15 SATURDAY

16 SUNDAY

WEEK 34

AUGUST

17 MONDAY

18 TUESDAY

19 WEDNESDAY

20 THURSDAY   *New Moon*

21 FRIDAY

22 SATURDAY   First day of Ramadân (subject to sighting of the moon)

23 SUNDAY

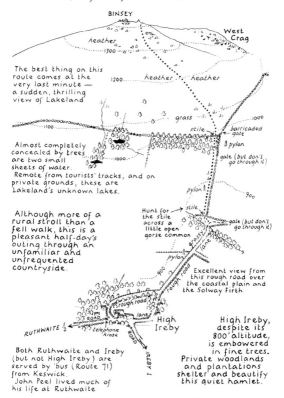

Binsey 7

THE SUMMIT

The summit is the best part of the fell, taking the form of a small ridge surmounted by a great heap of stones (in fact a tumulus) with an Ordnance Survey column alongside and a well-built wall shelter at the foot of the tumble of stones on the north side. There is a lower cairn to the north-west. With the added attraction of an excellent view, this summit is worthy of a greater mountain than Binsey.

DESCENTS: All routes of descent are simple. At West Crag there is a little roughness. *In mist, bearings can be taken at the summit: the Survey column is east of the tumulus, and the shelter north.*

Binsey Lodge (which is not in sight) is reached by aiming for Over Water (which is).

On the top of Binsey.........

..... Prehistoric Tumulus and Ancient Briton

WEEK 35

AUGUST

24 MONDAY

25 TUESDAY

26 WEDNESDAY

27 THURSDAY　　　　　　　　　　　　　　　　　　　　　　　*First Quarter*

28 FRIDAY

29 SATURDAY

30 SUNDAY

Whin Rigg 1755'

from Strands

from the north-east (on the approach from Illgill Head)

WEEK 36

AUGUST/SEPTEMBER

31 MONDAY Summer Bank Holiday, UK (exc. Scotland)

1 TUESDAY

2 WEDNESDAY

3 THURSDAY

4 FRIDAY *Full Moon*

5 SATURDAY

6 SUNDAY Father's Day, Australia and New Zealand

WEEK 37

SEPTEMBER

---

7 MONDAY
Holiday, USA (Labor Day)
Holiday, Canada (Labour Day)

---

8 TUESDAY

---

9 WEDNESDAY

---

10 THURSDAY

---

11 FRIDAY

---

12 SATURDAY
Last Quarter

---

13 SUNDAY

Whin Rigg 2

NATURAL FEATURES

No mountain in Lakeland, not even Great Gable nor Blencathra nor the Langdale Pikes, can show a grander front than Whin Rigg, modest in elevation though the latter is, and so little known that most visitors to the district will not have heard the name.   Wastwater Screes, of course, is a place familiar to many; Whin Rigg is the southern terminus of the shattered ridge above Wast Water, beyond the screes, where the great grey cliffs have resisted erosion and rise in gigantic towers over the foot of the lake to culminate finally in a small shapely summit, a proud eyrie indeed. This savage scene is tempered and given a rare beauty by the blending of dark waters and rich woodlands that form the base of every view of the soaring buttresses — but there is no denying the steepness and severity of its precipices and chasms. This is one fellside that walkers can write off at a glance as having no access for them.

The opposite flank, to the east, is, in a contrast absolute, gently graded and everywhere grassy; it descends dully to the narrow branch-valley of Miterdale, a lovely and almost secret fold of the hills, unspoiled, serene. The southern ridge of the fell declines to the long grassy shoulder of Irton Fell and the rocky Irton Pike, now largely under timber; beyond is a pleasant countryside watered by the Esk and the Irt, both of them fed by Whin Rigg, and then, to the far horizon, is the sea.

It is along this ridge that walkers may find a simple way to the summit and so look down on the lake from the cairn, and, by going a little further, between the vertical walls of the tremendous gullies. This is dramatic scenery, quite unique, and with an abiding impression of grandeur that makes the ascent of Whin Rigg a walk to be remembered and thought about often.

Whin Rigg 5

ASCENT FROM NETHER WASDALE
1600 feet of ascent : 2 miles from Woodhow farm

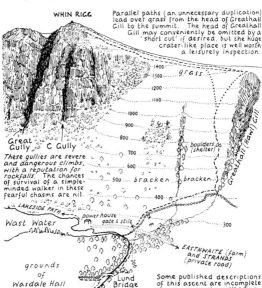

Parallel paths (an unnecessary duplication) lead over grass from the head of Greathall Gill to the summit. The head of Greathall Gill may conveniently be omitted by a 'short cut' if desired, but the huge crater-like place is well worth a leisurely inspection.

These gullies are severe and dangerous climbs, with a reputation for rockfalls. The chances of survival of a simpleminded walker in these fearful chasms are nil.

There is no difficulty in identifying Woodhow: it is the only farm on the roadside between Wasdale Hall and Strands.

The new power-house at the foot of the lake, expelling hot air from its grills, is a useful drying-out place for wet walkers.

Some published descriptions of this ascent are incomplete or even seriously misleading. The climb starts *not directly from the lake*, but after a walk away from it, alongside an ascending wall, for almost half a mile, to Greathall Gill (better known as Hawl Gill). The Gill, a tremendous slice cut out of the fellside, is a favourite hunting-ground of geologists. A path zigzags upwards here but ceases at the upper limit of bracken.

looking east

The reward for this climb comes not from the doing of it but from the unique, beautiful and inspiring situation to which it leads: the top of the towering crags and gullies of the Screes, a scene without a counterpart elsewhere.

WEEK 38

SEPTEMBER

14 MONDAY

15 TUESDAY

16 WEDNESDAY

17 THURSDAY

18 FRIDAY *New Moon*

19 SATURDAY Jewish New Year (Rosh Hashanah)

20 SUNDAY

WEEK 39

SEPTEMBER

21 MONDAY Eid al Fitr, Ramadân ends

22 TUESDAY Autumnal Equinox

23 WEDNESDAY

24 THURSDAY

25 FRIDAY

26 SATURDAY *First Quarter*

27 SUNDAY

Whin Rigg 8

RIDGE ROUTE

To ILLGILL HEAD, 1983': 1⅓ miles : NE
Depression at 1550': 450 feet of ascent
Easy walking; thrilling views

The best scenery and the excitement occur in the first half-mile, and this is a section to linger over as long as time permits. Photographers will go frantic here, but cameras cannot capture the magnificence of the gullies and aretes plunging down to Wast Water. A grass path links the summits, with a few variations to choose from in the depression; most walkers, however, will prefer to follow the escarpment as closely as possible. Photographers are urged to save one exposure for the view of Wasdale Head from the further cairn on Illgill Head.

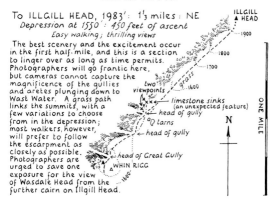

The two viewpoints
indicated on the diagram
(as seen from the north-east,
i.e. the Illgill Head side)

That on the left forms a small peak on the brink of the escarpment, and is a prominent object on the ridge-walk. The other is a narrow arete (Broken Rib) going down from the ridge. Both places are easily visited.

Castle Crag

985'
approx.

from the south

WEEK 40

SEPTEMBER/OCTOBER

28 MONDAY   Day of Atonement (Yom Kippur)

29 TUESDAY   Michaelmas Day

30 WEDNESDAY

1 THURSDAY

2 FRIDAY

3 SATURDAY   Festival of Tabernacles (Succoth), First Day

4 SUNDAY   *Full Moon*

WEEK 41

OCTOBER

5 MONDAY

6 TUESDAY

7 WEDNESDAY

8 THURSDAY

9 FRIDAY

10 SATURDAY   Festival of Tabernacles (Succoth), Eighth Day

11 SUNDAY   *Last Quarter*

Castle Crag 2

NATURAL FEATURES

Perhaps, to be strictly correct, Castle Crag should be regarded not as a separate fell but as a protuberance on the rough breast of Low Scawdel, occurring almost at the foot of the slope and remote from the ultimate summit of High Spy far above and out of sight. Castle Crag has no major geographical function — it is not a watershed, does not persuade the streams of Scawdel from their predestined purpose of joining the Derwent and interrupts only slightly the natural fall of the fell to Borrowdale: on the general scale of the surrounding heights it is of little significance.

Yet Castle Crag is so magnificently independent, so ruggedly individual, so aggressively unashamed of its lack of inches, that less than justice would be done by relegating it to a paragraph in the High Spy chapter. If its top is below 1000 feet, which is doubtful (no official height having been determined), it is the only fell below 1000 feet in this series of books that is awarded the full treatment; a distinction well earned.

Castle Crag conforms to no pattern. It is an obstruction in the throat of Borrowdale, confining passage therein to the width of a river and a road, hiding what lies beyond, defying cultivation. Its abrupt pyramid, richly wooded from base almost to summit but bare at the top, is a wild tangle of rough steep ground, a place of crags and scree and tumbled boulders, of quarry holes and spoil dumps, of confusion and disorder. But such is the artistry of nature, such is the mellowing influence of the passing years, that the scars of disarray and decay have been transformed in a romantic harmony, cloaked by a canopy of trees and a carpet of leaves. There are lovely copses of silver birch by the crystal-clear river, magnificent specimens of Scots pine higher up. Naked of trees, Castle Crag would be ugly; with them, it has a sylvan beauty unsurpassed, unique.

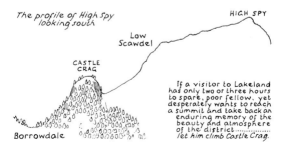

The profile of High Spy looking south

HIGH SPY

Low Scawdel

CASTLE CRAG

Borrowdale

If a visitor to Lakeland has only two or three hours to spare, poor fellow, yet desperately wants to reach a summit and take back an enduring memory of the beauty and atmosphere of the district............ let him climb Castle Crag.

Castle Crag 3

The summit-quarry

The pedestrian path to the top goes up the grass on the right

summit

Quarries and caves of Castle Crag

In addition to the summit-quarry, which is open to the sky and obvious to all who climb the fell, the steep flank above the Derwent is pitted with cuttings and caverns and levels, every hole having its tell-tale spoilheap, but the scars of this former industrial activity are largely concealed by a screen of trees and not generally noticed. Much of this flank is precipitous, the ground everywhere is very rough, and the vertically-hewn walls of naked stone are dangerous traps for novice explorers.

Of these quarries the best known is High Hows, the debris of which is passed on the riverside walk from Grange to Rosthwaite. A detour up the quarry road leads to a series of caverns, which for older walkers have a nostalgic interest: here in one of them Millican Dalton, a mountaineering adventurer and a familiar character in the district between the wars (died 1947, aged 80) furnished a home for his summer residence, using an adjacent cave at a higher level (the 'Attic') as sleeping quarters. Note here his lettering cut in the rock at the entrance — 'Don't!! Waste words, jump to conclusions'

The Attic

Millican's Cave

WEEK 42

OCTOBER

12 MONDAY   Holiday, Canada (Thanksgiving)
                                        Holiday, USA (Columbus Day)

13 TUESDAY

14 WEDNESDAY

15 THURSDAY

16 FRIDAY

17 SATURDAY

18 SUNDAY   *New Moon*

Castle Crag 7

THE SUMMIT

The summit is circular in plan, about 60 yards in diameter, and a perfect natural stronghold. Even today, one man in possession, armed with a stick, could prevent its occupation by others whatever their number, there being one strategic point (the place of access to the top) where passage upward is restricted to single-file traffic. Authorities agree that there was once a fort here, probably early British, but it needs a trained eye to trace any earthworks — which, in any case, must have been severely disturbed by an old quarry that has cut a big slice out of the summit and, be it noted, constitutes an unprotected danger. Photographers (who have a habit of taking backward steps when composing their pictures) should take care lest they suddenly vanish.

The highest point is a boss of rock, and this is crowned by a professionally-made round flat-topped cairn, below which, set in the rock, is a commemorative tablet: a war memorial to the men of Borrowdale, effective and imaginative. A stunted larch grows alongside, clinging for dear life to the rim of a crag, and better specimens surround the perimeter.

DESCENTS: For the ordinary walker there is only one way on and off, and this is on the south side, by a clump of larch, where a clear track descends between the edge of the quarry (right) and a cutting (left) to the flat top of the spoil-heap, at the end of which a ramp on the right inclines in zigzags to the grass below. Here, if bound for Rosthwaite, climb the wall on the left; for Grange the way continues down, crossing two walls by stiles, to the old Rigghead road.

ENVIRONS OF THE SUMMIT

WEEK 43

OCTOBER

19 MONDAY

20 TUESDAY

21 WEDNESDAY

22 THURSDAY

23 FRIDAY

24 SATURDAY — United Nations Day

25 SUNDAY — British Summer Time ends

Bakestall

2189'

not named on
1" Ordnance
Survey maps

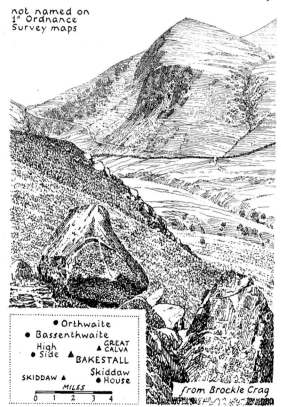

from Brockle Crag

- Orthwaite
- Bassenthwaite
- High Side   ▲ GREAT CALVA
            ▲ BAKESTALL
SKIDDAW ▲   • Skiddaw House

MILES
0 1 2 3 4

WEEK 44

OCTOBER/NOVEMBER

26 MONDAY
First Quarter
Holiday, New Zealand (Labour Day)
Holiday, Republic of Ireland

27 TUESDAY

28 WEDNESDAY

29 THURSDAY

30 FRIDAY

31 SATURDAY Hallowe'en

1 SUNDAY All Saints' Day

WEEK 45

NOVEMBER

---

2 MONDAY *Full Moon*

---

3 TUESDAY

---

4 WEDNESDAY

---

5 THURSDAY *Guy Fawkes' Day*

---

6 FRIDAY

---

7 SATURDAY

---

8 SUNDAY Remembrance Sunday, UK

Bakestall 2

NATURAL FEATURES

Even the most diligent student of maps of Lakeland is not likely to have noticed the name of Bakestall and few walkers will have heard of it. Bakestall (the name of a summit rather than of a fell) is a rough raised platform on the sprawling north flank of Skiddaw, merely a halt in the easy slopes and barely qualifying for recognition as a separate top. It would pass almost without comment but for its command of a scene of extra-ordinary interest: a unique combination of natural features that arrests the attention all the more because it is unexpected, startling and seemingly out of place amongst the smooth heathery uplands all around. The summit is perched high above a steepening slope from which has been scooped an enormous hollow, as though a giant hand had clawed at and ripped away the fellside, leaving a rim of crags along the line of cleavage. This escarpment, a rising horseshoe of cliffs half-a-mile in length, is Dead Crags, a dark yet colourful rampart of buttresses and jutting aretes patched a vivid green with bilberry and brown and purple with ling. But grander even than this strange and silent crater are the magnificent waterfalls in the precipitous wooded ravine at its base, where Dash Beck, issuing from the vast waste of Skiddaw Forest, leaps exultantly at its first glimpse of gentle pastures and plunges over the lip in a series of falls, one following another in a mighty torment of roaring and thrashing waters — the finest spectacle of its kind in the district. This is Whitewater Dash, also known as Dash Falls, a tremendous sight in spate, when the thunder of its great cataracts can be heard miles away down the valley. The brave little road to Skiddaw House, climbing sinuously in and out of the hollow to disappear over the skyline, is the one evidence of man, but instead of intruding, as roads so often do, this desolate track merely adds to the loneliness of the scene. On the west, Bakestall is clearly defined by Dead Beck, which flows down a rough and rocky gutter to join Dash Beck en route for Bassenthwaite Lake.

1: The summit
2: Ridge continuing to Skiddaw
3: Cockup
4: Broad End
5: Dead Crags
6: Terminal cliff
7: Dash Falls
8: Dash Beck
9: Tod Gill
10: Dead Beck
11: Skiddaw Forest

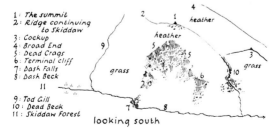

looking south

WEEK 46

NOVEMBER

9 MONDAY   *Last Quarter*

10 TUESDAY

11 WEDNESDAY   Holiday, USA (Veterans' Day)
                                                   Holiday, Canada (Remembrance Day)

12 THURSDAY

13 FRIDAY

14 SATURDAY

15 SUNDAY

Bakestall 4

ASCENT FROM THE ROAD TO SKIDDAW HOUSE
900 feet of ascent : ⅔ mile from Dash Falls
(1750 feet, 4⅔ miles from High Side or Bassenthwaite Village)

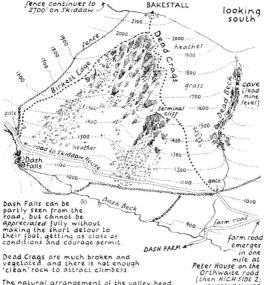

Dash Falls can be partly seen from the road, but cannot be appreciated fully without making the short detour to their foot, getting as close as conditions and courage permit.

Dead Crags are much broken and vegetated, and there is not enough 'clean' rock to attract climbers.

The natural arrangement of the valley-head, although on no great scale, offers an excellent composition for an artist (stationed near Dash farm) and a perfect object-lesson for a geography class.

Two routes are given, that by Birkett Edge being the better for views of Dead Crags and convenient for an easy visit to Dash Falls. (This is also, incidentally, the best way to Skiddaw from any point on the rough Skiddaw House road). The more direct route, going up steeply between the terminal cliff and Dead Beck from the gate in the intake wall, is less interesting; note that this route should not be used for descent in mist, when only sheer good luck could prevent one from running foul of crags.

Bakestall 5

THE SUMMIT

The summits of the Northern Fells are not, as a rule, distinguished by handsome and imposing cairns, due more to a lack of suitable building material in the vicinity, no doubt, than to a lack of industry on the part of visitors, and the uncharacteristic summit of Bakestall, where good rough rock outcropping amongst the heather has served to provide a solid and substantial column, is nostalgically refreshing to a walker whose preference is for rugged tops. This cairn does not occupy the highest point of the summit (which occurs at the angle of the fence) but is 100 yards to the north at a better place of vantage overlooking a very pleasant pastoral scene: the Dash valley.

DESCENTS: All descents must of necessity be to the road to Skiddaw House skirting the base of the fell, and this is quickly reached by following first the fence down Birkett Edge (detour to the left to see the combe of Dead Crags) and then a short wall. In mist, there is no safe alternative, but in clear weather the steep slope may be descended directly to the rim of Dead Crags (taking care not to panic the sheep grazing there) where a rough track will be found slanting down on the right to Birkett Edge.

If it is desired to locate the old mine level in the Dead Beck ravine on the way down to the road descend the easy slope of heather northwest to the beck. The 'cave' is in the far bank, 50 yards below the first rowan trees and a few feet above the stream-bed. The ravine becomes too rough to follow in comfort lower down but the road may be reached by a detour on the steep grass of either bank. It should be noted that on this route nothing will be seen of Dead Crags or Dash Falls, the cave and ravine, although interesting, being poor compensation.

A: Dead Crags
B: Birkett Edge
C: Dead Beck
D: to Skiddaw

WEEK 47

NOVEMBER

16 MONDAY　　　　　　　　　　　　　　　　　　　　　　　　　　*New Moon*

17 TUESDAY

18 WEDNESDAY

19 THURSDAY

20 FRIDAY

21 SATURDAY

22 SUNDAY

WEEK 48

NOVEMBER

23 MONDAY

24 TUESDAY *First Quarter*

25 WEDNESDAY

26 THURSDAY Holiday, USA (Thanksgiving Day)

27 FRIDAY

28 SATURDAY

29 SUNDAY First Sunday in Advent

Bakestall 10

The old mine level in the ravine of Dead Beck (Cave entrance 5' x 3', but flooded)

Dash Falls
(Whitewater Dash on Ordnance maps)

There are many finer individual waterfalls in Lakeland, but for a grand succession of falls the first place must undoubtedly be given to Dash Falls.
  Little more than half the total height is shown in the illustration.

WEEK 49

NOVEMBER/DECEMBER

30 MONDAY　　　　　　　　　　　　　　　　　　　　　　St. Andrew's Day

1 TUESDAY

2 WEDNESDAY　　　　　　　　　　　　　　　　　　　　　　*Full Moon*

3 THURSDAY

4 FRIDAY

5 SATURDAY

6 SUNDAY

WEEK 50

DECEMBER

7 MONDAY

8 TUESDAY

9 WEDNESDAY *Last Quarter*

10 THURSDAY

11 FRIDAY

12 SATURDAY

13 SUNDAY   Jewish Festival of Chanukah, First Day

Outerside 2

NATURAL FEATURES

The valley of Coledale, coming down straight as an arrow to Braithwaite, is deeply enclosed by a continuous horseshoe rim of high summits, from Causey Pike round to Grisedale Pike, but while the latter descends uncompromisingly in a very steep and unbroken slope, the opposite ridge of Causey Pike is accompanied by a lower and parallel ridge like an inner balcony, the fall to the valley being thereby interrupted. The main eminence on this subsidiary ridge is the abrupt summit of Outerside, and its position is such that it looks down into the vast pit of the head of Coledale and up to the exciting skyline of the surrounding ring of peaks. This secondary ridge ends in Barrow, overlooking Newlands, and above a thousand feet has a rich heather cover, which gives to the upper expanses a gloomy and forbidding appearance that is belied by a close acquaintance. Between Outerside and Barrow, but out of alignment like a dog's back leg, rises the lesser height of Stile End, which, seen from the Braithwaite approach, forms a noble pyramid.

Outerside springs quite steeply from the abyss of Coledale, and in a less distinctive company it would attract much attention. As it is, visitors rarely tread its pleasant summit.

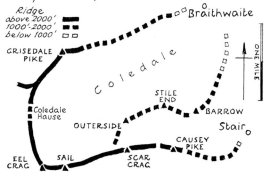

Outerside 5

ASCENT FROM BRAITHWAITE
1650 feet of ascent : 2½ miles

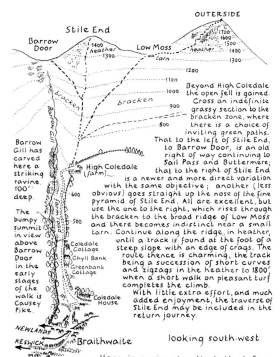

looking south-west

Beyond High Coledale the open fell is gained. Cross an indefinite grassy section to the bracken zone, where there is a choice of inviting green paths. That to the left of Stile End, to Barrow Door, is an old right of way continuing to Sail Pass and Buttermere; that to the right of Stile End is a newer and more direct variation with the same objective; another (less obvious) goes straight up the nose of the fine pyramid of Stile End. All are excellent, but use the one to the right, which rises through the bracken to the broad ridge of Low Moss and there becomes indistinct near a small tarn. Continue along the ridge, in heather, until a track is found at the foot of a steep slope with an edge of crags. The route thence is charming, the track being a succession of short curves and zigzags in the heather to 1800', when a short walk on pleasant turf completes the climb.

With little extra effort, and much added enjoyment, the traverse of Stile End may be included in the return journey.

Here is a simple climb that few walkers ever bother to do; and by this omission they deny themselves a lot of pleasure and a rewarding introduction to the grand circle of hills around Coledale.

WEEK 51

DECEMBER

14 MONDAY

15 TUESDAY

16 WEDNESDAY   *New Moon*

17 THURSDAY

18 FRIDAY   Islamic New Year (subject to sighting of the moon)

19 SATURDAY

20 SUNDAY

WEEK 52

DECEMBER

21 MONDAY   Winter Solstice

---

22 TUESDAY

---

23 WEDNESDAY

---

24 THURSDAY   *First Quarter*
                                                                                  Christmas Eve

---

25 FRIDAY   Christmas Day
                          Holiday, UK, Republic of Ireland, Canada, USA,
                                                          Australia and New Zealand

---

26 SATURDAY   Boxing Day (St. Stephen's Day)

---

27 SUNDAY

Outerside 6

THE SUMMIT

From the east the highest point is reached at the end of a gradual incline; from the west it appears abruptly at the top of a rising pavement of embedded rocks: here a few loose stones form a small cairn. The Coledale edge is close by, falling away sharply in an escarpment, and in mist this edge may be followed as a guide to a track down the eastern ridge, the only path off the top.

DESCENTS: The escarpment can be negotiated, with care, on initially steep ground if a direct way down into Coledale is desired, but there is little point in this since Coledale leads only to Braithwaite, which is more quickly and attractively reached by the eastern ridge (watch for a track in the heather) and then by a good path slanting down to the left below the rise to Stile End. For Stair, too, the eastern ridge is best, turning down to the right at the depression to join the Stonycroft mine road.

Sail Pass (left), Sail and Eel Crag from Outerside

WEEK 1 2010

DECEMBER/JANUARY

---

28 MONDAY   Holiday, UK, Canada

---

29 TUESDAY

---

30 WEDNESDAY

---

31 THURSDAY   *Full Moon*
                                             New Year's Eve

---

1 FRIDAY   New Year's Day
   Holiday, UK, Republic of Ireland, Canada, USA, Australia and New Zealand

---

2 SATURDAY   Holiday, Scotland and New Zealand

---

3 SUNDAY

Outerside 8

RIDGE ROUTE

To BARROW, 1494': 1¼ miles: ENE, then SE and ENE
Depressions at 1380' and 1270'
400 feet of ascent
Rough walking in heather. Avoid Stile End in mist.

If the ridge is to be followed conscientiously, the traverse of
Stile End must be included in this walk, although this middle
height can more easily be bypassed
between Low Moss and Barrow Door.
Starting down the eastern ridge,
keep always to the highest
ground ahead; on Stile End
this means a sharp turn
to the right.

Outerside from Stile End

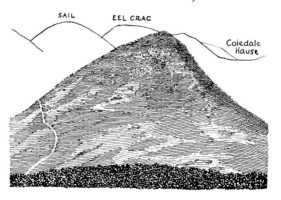